·T·H·E·
WIT'S
DICTIONARY

· T · H · E ·

WIT'S
DICTIONARY

COLIN BOWLES

Illustrated by
Peter Townsend

ANGUS & ROBERTSON PUBLISHERS

ANGUS & ROBERTSON PUBLISHERS
London . Sydney . Melbourne

First published in Australia by
Angus & Robertson Publishers in 1984
First published in the United Kingdom by
Angus & Robertson (UK) Ltd in 1984
Reprinted 1984, 1985

Copyright © Colin Bowles 1984

National Library of Australia
Cataloguing-in-publication data.
Bowles, Colin.
  The wit's dictionary.
  ISBN 0 207 14940 2.
  1. English language — Dictionaries.   2. Wit and
  humor.   I. Title.
423'.0207

Typeset in 11pt Goudy Old Style by Setrite Typesetters
Printed in Hong Kong

PREFACE

"The English language is like a juggernaut truck —
it goes on regardless."

Dr Robert Burchfield,
editor-in-chief,
Oxford English dictionaries

Any dictionary will tell you the definition of a word. But can it give you the true meaning?

The Wit's Dictionary goes beyond definition. It takes you backstage to see how our everyday words think and feel before they are dressed up and go out to perform.

We live in an age of doubletalk. We are blinded and deafened by the propaganda of the politicos, the nuances of the media and the jargon of technology, frustrated by the endless gobbledegook that hides the truth as it really is. Words themselves have become a disguise.

So here, then, is The Wit's Dictionary — a dictionary that goes beyond mere definition and gives you the real meaning of the words you hear every day. Some are humorous, some poignant, some will make you stop and think.

Come behind the scenes of the English language — for reference, for sanity, or just for fun. English will never seem the same again.

abasement (n.) an act of faith when a man decides he is not God. [*Oliver Wendell Holmes*]

absolute (n.) the limit of our conceptions. [*orig.*]

abstract art (n.) a product of the untalented, sold by the unprincipled, to the utterly bewildered. [*Al Capp*]

Academy Awards (n.) a gold rush in dinner jackets. [*adapted from Boris Morros*]

accent (n.) something other people have. [*orig.*]

accomplishment (n.) one per cent inspiration and 99 per cent perspiration. [*adapted from Thomas Edison*]

accountant (n.) someone who can put two and two together to make a living. [*orig.*]

achievement (n.) the death of endeavour and the birth of disgust. [*Ambrose Bierce*]

acquaintance (n.) a person whom we know well enough to borrow from, but not well enough to lend to. [*Ambrose Bierce*]

acting (n.) the ability to keep an audience from coughing. [*Ralph Richardson*]

actor (n.) a man who can walk to the side of the stage, peer into the wings filled with dust, other actors, stagehands, old clothes and other claptrap and say, "What a lovely view there is from this window." [*Variety*]

actress (n.) a lady, who, if you ain't talkin' about her, ain't listenin'. [*adapted from Marlon Brando*]

Adam's apple (n.) a protuberance in the throat of man, thoughtfully provided by nature to keep the rope in place. [Ambrose Bierce]

Adam's rib (n.) the original bone of contention. [Oliver Wendell Holmes]

ad libber (n.) a man who stays up all night memorising spontaneous jokes. [Wall Street Journal]

administration (n.) the art of looking for trouble, finding it whether it exists or not, diagnosing it incorrectly and applying the wrong remedy. [adapted from Sir Ernest Benn]

admiral (n.) a general at sea. [L. L. Levinson]

admiration (n.) our polite recognition of another's resemblance to ourselves. [Ambrose Bierce]

ad nauseam (adv.) (Latin) a commercial for indigestion tablets. [orig.]

adolescence (n.) the period when children are certain they will never be as dumb as their parents. [anon.]

adolescent (n.) someone who is well informed about anything he doesn't have to study. [anon.]

adult (n.) an obsolete child. [Dr Seuss]

adultery (n.) doing the right thing with the wrong person. [orig.]

adult western (n.) one in which the hero loves his horse better than the girl, but he's worried about it. [Arthur Murphy]

adversity (n.) the state in which a man most easily becomes acquainted with himself, being especially free from admirers then. [Samuel Johnson]

advertising (n.) the science of arresting the human intelligence long enough to get money from it. [Stephen Leacock]

advertising agency (n.) 85 per cent confusion and 15 per cent commission [Fred Allen]

advertising executive (n.) yessir, nosir, ulcer. [Lee Bristol]

advice (n.) something we test out on others to see if it really works. [orig.]

aesthete (n.) a guy who can listen to the "William Tell Overture" without thinking of "The Lone Ranger". [adapted from Jack Perlis]

agnostic (n.) a person who only prays as a last resort. [orig.]

advertising executive . . . yessir, nosir, ulcer.

agreeable (*adj.*) someone who agrees with you. [*Benjamin Disraeli*]

alcohol (*n.*) liquid ego. [*orig.*]

alcoholic (*n.*) a guy who tries to pull himself out of trouble with a corkscrew. [*Ed Baldwin*]

alimony (*n.*) a system whereby, if two people make a mistake, one of them continues to pay for it. [*Peggy Joyce*]

alliance (*n.*) a union of two thieves who have their hands so deeply in each other's pockets that they cannot separately plunder a third. [*Ambrose Bierce*]

alter ego (*n.*) a conceited priest. [*Playboy*]

ambassador (*n.*) a spy with a title. [*Napoleon*]

ambidextrous (*adj.*) someone who can pick both nostrils at the same time. [*orig.*]

America (*n.*) the best half-educated country in the world. [*Nicholas Murray Butler*]

Americans (*n.*) people who feel rich because they charge each other so much. [*anon.*]

amulet (*n.*) a Danish omelette. [*anon.*]

anarchist (*n.*) someone who has been kicked out of the Communist Party. [*orig.*]

anatomy (*n.*) something everybody has, but it looks better on a girl. [*Bruce Raeburn*]

anger (*n.*) temporary madness. [*Saint Basil*]

angler (*n.*) a man who sits around on river banks doing nothing because his wife won't let him sit around doing nothing at home. [*Irish News*]

annulment (*n.*) a romance in which the hero dies in the first chapter. [*anon.*]

anonymous (*adj.*) a married author writing something about women. [*anon.*]

Antarctica (*n.*) Snowman's land. [*L. L. Levinson*]

anthem (*n.*) a commercial about a country. [*orig.*]

anticlimax (*n.*) when life tickles our nose but we are unable to sneeze. [*orig.*]

antique (*n.*) something no-one would want if there were two of them. [*anon.*]

antique furniture (*n.*) furniture that is paid for. [*anon.*]

apartheid (n.) a society where things are either black or white. [orig.]

apathy (n.) the condition of a person who has sat on the fence for so long that the iron has entered into his soul. [adapted from Lloyd George]

aperitif (n.) dentures. [anon.]

apology (n.) when the heart takes over from the mouth. [orig.]

abject apology (n.) putting sugar on your words before you eat them. [orig.]

appeal (n.) when one court is asked to show its contempt for another court. [Finley Peter Dunne]

appeaser (n.) someone who feeds a crocodile hoping it will eat him last. [Winston Churchill]

Arab (n.) a Greek on a camel. [orig.]

archaeologist (n.) the best sort of husband for a woman to have: the older she gets, the more interested he is in her. [Agatha Christie]

archaeology (n.) digging up the past. [Leonard Woolley]

archbishop (n.) a Christian who has attained a rank superior to that of Christ. [H. L. Mencken]

argument (n.) a conversation between two people with a highly developed faculty for shouting and a greatly retarded faculty for listening. [orig.]

aristocrat (n.) someone who thinks he is Napoleon during the week and Jesus Christ on Sundays. [orig.]

armed conflict (n.) a continuation of dialogue by other means. [Karl von Clausewitz]

army (n.) a body of men assembled to rectify the mistakes of the diplomats. [Josephus Daniels]

arson (n.) a fire caused by the friction between the fire insurance policy and the mortgage. [anon.]

arsonist (n.) a man with a burning desire. [Ethel Meglin]

art (n.) breaking a hole in the subconscious and fishing there. [Robert Beverly Hale]

arthritis (n.) twinges on the hinges. [G. B. Howard]

artistic temperament (n.) a disease that afflicts amateurs. [*G. K. Chesterton*]

assassination (n.) an extreme form of censorship. [*George Bernard Shaw*]

atheist (n.) someone who has faith that there is nothing to have faith in. [*orig.*]

atom (n.) a subdivision of matter that is likely to be the death of the subdivision business. [*L. L. Levinson*]

auditor (n.) someone who goes round after the battle bayoneting the wounded. [*anon.*]

Australia (n.) an amalgam of eight states with independent governments united by mutual resentment. [*orig.*]

Australian (n.) someone who is too drunk to feel his sunburn. [*orig.*]

Australian novel (n.) a story in which boy meets girl, boy gets girl, goes down to the pub with his mates to celebrate and never comes back. [*orig.*]

author (n.) someone who gets words wholesale and sells them retail. [*adapted from Anthony Trollope*]

autobiography (n.) an unrivalled vehicle for telling the truth about other people. [*Philip Guedalla*]

automobile (n.) a guided missile. [*anon.*]

awe (n.) respect with the mouth open. [*L. L. Levinson*]

baby (n.) an alimentary canal with a loud voice at one end and no sense of responsibility at the other. [*Elizabeth Adamson*]

baby-sitter (n.) a person who gets paid to watch television. [*anon.*]

bachelor (n.) a man who believes it is better to have loved and lost than get up for the two a.m. feeding. [*anon.*]

confirmed bachelor (n.) a thing of beauty and a boy forever. [*Helen Rowland*]

bacillus (n.) a microbe on the make. [*Frank Scully*]

backbencher (n.) someone who is elected to insignificance. [*orig.*]

bagpipes (n.) an octopus with a kilt on. [*orig.*]

banal (adj.) a gigantic ordinary. [*orig.*]

bank (n.) an institution where you can borrow money if you can provide sufficient evidence to show you don't need it. [*Joe Lewis*]

banker (n.) a pawnbroker with a manicure. [*Jackson Parks*]

bankruptcy (n.) a legal proceeding in which you put your money in your back pocket and give your coat to your creditors. [*Paul Steiner*]

bank statement (n.) the mathematical confirmation of your suspicions. [*adapted from A. A. Latimer*]

banquet (n.) a $10 dinner served in sufficient numbers to enable the caterer to charge $50 for it. [*L. L. Levinson*]

baptism (*n.*) a spiritual sheep dip. [*John Grigg*]

barbecue (*n.*) smoke without fire. [*orig.*]

barmaid (*n.*) what the boys in the backroom will have. [*L. L. Levinson*]

barrister (*n.*) a person you hire when you've murdered somebody and you want it explained to the jury in the best possible light. [*anon.*]

bath mat (*n.*) a little rug wet children like to stand next to. [*anon.*]

beauty (*n.*) God's trademark in creation. [*Henry Ward Beecher*]

beauty parlour (*n.*) a stable where the doors are closed after the horse has bolted. [*orig.*]

bee (*n.*) nature's confectioner. [*John Cleveland*]

beggar (*n.*) a pest unkindly inflicted upon the suffering rich. [*Ambrose Bierce*]

belch (*n.*) the Australian national anthem. [*orig.*]

betting (*n.*) putting money on a horse to prevent it winning. [*adapted from Frank Richardson*]

Bible (*n.*) a prophet and lust account. [*orig.*]

bigamist (*n.*) a heavy Italian fog. [*anon.*]

bigamy (*n.*) two rites making a wrong. [*Bob Hope*]

bigotry (*n.*) the articulation of ignorance. [*orig.*]

big shot (*n.*) a little shot who kept shooting. [*Christopher Morley*]

biography (*n.*) a fate worse than death. [*anon.*]

birth control (*n.*) copulation without population. [*anon.*]

bitch (*n.*) a woman who treads all over a man's corns on the pretext of stepping up to kiss his lips. [*orig.*]

bitter (*adj.*) someone who has been bit. [*orig.*]

bitterness (*n.*) indigestion of the heart. [*orig.*]

bittersweet (*adj.*) the pleasure of regret. [*orig.*]

blancmange (*n.*) the highest peak in the Swiss Alps. [*anon.*]

blasé (*adj.*) determined apathy. [*orig.*]

book (*n.*) something with which to pass the time while waiting for the TV repairman to arrive. [*anon.*]

bookie (n.) a pickpocket who lets you use your own hands. [Henry Morgan]

bore (n.) a person who talks when you want him to listen. [Ambrose Bierce]

boss (n.) the man at the office who's late when you're early and early when you're late. [anon.]

bourgeoisie (n.) (French) people who are not poor enough to qualify for charity and not rich enough to make donations. [anon.]

bowling (n.) marbles for grown-ups. [L. L. Levinson]

bowser wowser (n.) a homosexual dog. [orig.]

Boxer Rebellion (n.) a big uprising in China in 1900 when boxers demanded stools to sit on between rounds. [orig.]

boxing (n.) picking up your teeth with gloves on. [Kin Hubbard]

boy (n.) a noise with dirt on it. [Punch]

brassiere (n.) an over-the-shoulder boulder holster. [anon.]

brave (adj.) the first man to swallow an oyster. [King James I]

brawl (n.) when someone else's emotions constrict your throat. [orig.]

breeding (n.) concealing how much we think of ourselves and how little we think of the other person. [Mark Twain]

brevity (n.) the soul of lingerie. [Dorothy Parker]

bridegroom (n.) something used at weddings. [anon.]

Brisbane (n.) Parramatta without the glamour. [orig.]

broker (n.) a bookmaker with a dictaphone. [orig.]

bronchitis (n.) a disease afflicting theatre audiences. [adapted from James Agate]

Buddha (n.) something you spread on bread. [orig.]

budget (n.) a method of worrying before you spend, as well as afterwards. [Dorothy Malone]

buffet (n.) when the hostess doesn't have enough chairs for everyone. [Earl Wilson]

bullfight (n.) an abattoir in fancy dress. [orig.]

bun (n.) the lowest form of wheat. [anon.]

bureaucracy (n.) a giant mechanism operated by pygmies. [Honoré de Balzac]

burial (*n.*) being put to
bed with a shovel.
[*L. L. Levinson*]

business (*n.*) the art of
extracting money from
another man's pocket
without resorting to violence.
[*Max Amsterdam*]

cabinet minister . . . someone who has climbed so high up the ladder of
success that all that is visible is his arse.

cabinet minister (n.) someone who has climbed so high up the ladder of success that all that is visible is his arse. [adapted from Francis Bacon]

café (n.) a failed restaurant. [orig.]

camel (n.) a horse planned by a committee. [Vogue]

Canberra (n.) the asylum for the inane. [orig.]

cannibal (n.) a guy who goes into a restaurant and orders the waiter. [Jack Benny]

canon (n.) a law that is fired with religion. [orig.]

capitalist (n.) someone who believes that profit is not without honour in his own country. [orig.]

career (n.) any job that starts after 10 a.m. [Franklin Jones]

Caruso, Robinson (n.) a great singer who lived on an island. [anon.]

cash (n.) a poor man's credit card. [Playboy]

caterpillar (n.) an upholstered worm. [Mickey Mouse]

Catholic (n.) a person who commits more sins than anyone else but gets no fun out of it. [anon.]

  Irish Catholic (n.) combustible mixture of guilt, dogma and hard liquor. [orig.]

cats (n.) the crabgrass in the lawn of civilisation. [Snoopy]

cauliflower (n.) a cabbage with a college education. [Mark Twain]

celebrity (n.) a person who is known for his well-knowness. [Daniel Boorstin]

cemetery (n.) an isolated suburban spot where mourners match lies, poets write at a target and stone cutters attempt to spell. [Ambrose Bierce]

censor (n.) someone who chews our meat for us and decides what we should spit out. [orig.]

champion (n.) someone who gets up when he can't. [Jack Dempsey]

chance (n.) God's pseudonym when he does not wish to sign the work. [Anatole France]

chandelier (n.) a light bulb that thinks it's Napoleon. [orig.]

chaperon (n.) the person chosen to accompany the daughter to protect the father's morals. [orig.]

character (n.) when you have the same ailments as the other person but refrain from mentioning it. [anon.]

charisma (n.) the red carnation in the buttonhole that makes up for the hole in the head. [orig.]

charismatic service (n.) a Mass that's trying to be a musical. [orig.]

charity (n.) a thing that begins at home and usually stays there. [Elbert Hubbard]

charm (n.) the glow within a woman that casts a becoming light on others. [John Mason Brown]

chaste (adj.) a girl who has not yet been caught up with. [anon.]

chastity (n.) the facile ability to keep the legs crossed. [orig.]

cheerfulness (n.) the principal ingredient in the composition of health. [Arthur Murphy]

cheese (n.) milk's leap towards immortality. [Clifton Fadiman]

child (n.) a lump bred up in darkness. [Thomas Kyd]

childhood (n.) the wisdom of youth before it's old enough to have opinions. [orig.]

chimpanzee (n.) God's first draft of a politician. [orig.]

chivalry (n.) a man's inclination to defend a woman against every man but himself. [anon.]

Chopin, Frederic a Polish composer and pianist who greatly extended the technical and expressive range of the pianoforte. He also greatly extended the trading hours, leading to the introduction of "late-night Chopin". [anon.]

Christian (n.) someone who is stoic in the face of another's misfortune. [Alexander Pope]

  true Christian (n.) a person who fears the public appearance more than he fears the lions. [Ned Rorem]

Christianity (n.) a heresy that grew into a superstition. [adapted from T. H. Huxley]

Christmas (n.) when Santa comes down the chimney and money goes up in smoke. [orig.]

church (n.) a place in which gentlemen who have never been to heaven brag about it to persons who will never get there. [H. L. Mencken]

church bazaar (n.) a fête worse than death. [orig.]

Church of England (n.) the infant Jesus in the arms of an English nanny. [orig.]

cigarettes (n.) killers that travel in packs. [Mary Ott]

circle (n.) a round straight line with a hole in the middle. [anon.]

city (n.) millions of people being lonely together. [Henry David Thoreau]

civilisation (n.) a race between education and catastrophe. [H. G. Wells]

civil servant (n.) someone promoted to high government office to supervise the distribution of the graft. [adapted from Mark Twain]

clairvoyant (n.) a person, commonly a woman, who has the power of seeing that which is invisible to her patron — namely, that he is a blockhead. [Ambrose Bierce]

classic (n.) something everybody wants to have read and no-one wants to read. [Mark Twain]

clear conscience (n.) a bad memory. [proverb]

cleavage (n.) something you can approve of and look down on at the same time. [W. Garnett]

clerk (n.) a simple machine for operating a pen. [orig.]

climate (n.) the weather in a foreign country. [orig.]

clock (n.) a machine that produces uniform seconds, minutes and hours on an assembly line pattern. [*Marshall McLuhan*]

cocktail party (n.) a gathering where olives are speared in the middle and friends are stabbed in the back. [*anon.*]

coffee (n.) toasted milk. [*Christopher Fry*]

coincide (n.) what you do when it starts raining. [*anon.*]

coined (adj.) humane, as in "He was always coined to animals." [*anon.*]

college (n.) a place where we pass from adolescence to adultery. [*Professor R. Barry*]

committee (n.) a group that usually consists of five people — one who does all the work, three who pat him on the back, and one who apologises for his absence. [*orig.*]

communism (n.) an intellectual argument that makes it a moral duty for your inferiors to remain peasants. [*orig.*]

communist (n.) a person who has given up all hope of becoming a capitalist. [*anon.*]

competition (n.) the battle in which incompetence dies. [*anon.*]

compromise (n.) an agreement whereby both parties get what neither of them wants. [*anon.*]

conceit (n.) God's gift to little men. [*Bruce Barton*]

concentration (n.) the ability to do your son's homework while he is watching television. [*Terry McCormick*]

concerto (n.) a fight between a piano and a pianist [*orig.*]

conductor (n.) a man, dressed in a magician's outfit, who is deluded enough to think that by waving a wand at an orchestra he can make it play. [*orig.*]

conference (n.) a gathering of important people who singly can do nothing, but together can decide that nothing can be done. [*Fred Allen*]

confessional (n.) a spiritual dustbin. [*orig.*]

confidence (n.) the cocky feeling you get before you collide with reality. [*anon.*]

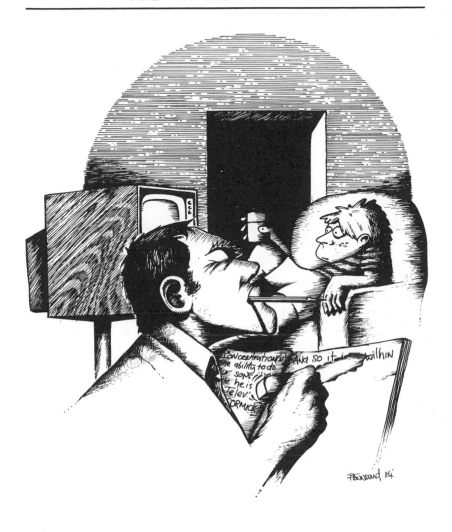

concentration . . . the ability to do your son's homework while he is watching television.

confiscate (*v.*) to rightfully assume another's property when he is unable to stop you taking it. [*orig.*]

conformist (*n.*) someone who is too lazy to think and too tired to get up. [*orig.*]

conformity (*n.*) something you can practise without making a spectacle of yourself. [*anon.*]

conscience (*n.*) the inner voice that warns us that somebody may be watching. [*H. L. Mencken*]

conservative (*n.*) someone who believes that nothing should be done for the first time. [*Alfred Wiggam*]

consistency (*n.*) the last refuge of the unimaginative. [*Oscar Wilde*]

consommé (*n.*) the exultant cry of a French bridegroom. [*Playboy*]

consultant (*n.*) someone who knows less about your business than you, but who gets more out of it by telling you what he knows than you do if you make it work the right way instead of doing what he tells you. [*anon.*]

consultation (*n.*) a meeting doctors have to pass the time while the patient dies. [*orig.*]

consumer (*n.*) a shopper who is sore about something. [*Harold Coffin*]

contentment (*n.*) something to do, something to love and something to hope for. [*anon.*]

contract (*n.*) an agreement to do something if nothing happens to prevent it. [*L. L. Levinson*]

convalescent (*n.*) a patient who is still alive. [*Dr Leo Michel*]

convention (*n.*) a place where all the normal conventions are forgotten. [*L. L. Levinson*]

convert (*n.*) someone who has been bullied into piety. [*orig.*]

cooperation (*n.*) doing with a smile what you are forced to do. [*anon.*]

coquette (*n.*) a girl who thinks she will have a baby if she kisses boys, and doesn't care. [*orig.*]

corporation (*n.*) an artificial person created by law to prey upon real things. [*Henry Waldorf Francis*]

cost-of-living index (*n.*) a list of numbers which proves that high prices are not expensive. [*Richard Weiss*]

counsel (n.) advice with a price tag. [L. L. Levinson]

country town (n.) a place where all the lights dim on the main street when you plug in your electric razor. [adapted from Paul Osborne]

courage (n.) the ability to stand up and speak, and the ability to sit down and listen. [anon.]

courtesy (n.) a form of polite behaviour practised by civilised people when they have time. [anon.]

courtship (n.) a period of time during which the girl decides if she can do better. [anon.]

coward (n.) someone who, in a perilous emergency, thinks with his legs. [Ambrose Bierce]

credit card (n.) a laminated loan shark. [Andrew Waterfield]

creditor (n.) a person who lends you a hand and then refuses to let go. [orig.]

preferential creditor (n.) the first person to be told there's no money left. [Financial Times]

cremation (n.) zombie flambée. [orig.]

crêpes suzette (n.) (French) pancakes with pyromania. [orig.]

criminal (n.) a person with predatory instincts who has not sufficient capital to form a corporation. [Howard Scott]

critic (n.) a failed author. [anon.]

croquet (n.) the polo of senility. [Jimmy Cannon]

crucifix (n.) a brand of glue. [orig.]

cult (n.) dogmatism chasing a catechism. [orig.]

culture (n.) what your butcher would have if he were a surgeon. [Mary P. Poole]

curve (n.) the loveliest distance between two points. [Mae West]

cynic (n.) a man who found out when he was ten that there was no Santa Claus, and he's still disappointed. [James Cozzens]

cynicism (n.) disappointed idealism. [Henry Kemmelman]

dachshund (n.) (German) a little dog, half-a-dog high and a dog-and-a-half long. [*Mary Ellen Herbert*]

dancing (n.) poetry of the foot. [*John Dryden*]

darling (n.) a woman's maiden name. [*anon.*]

Darwin (n.) a hot dusty city standing on the edge of the Cultural Desert. [*orig.*]

Darwin breakfast (n.) a T-bone steak, a carton of stubbies and a dog. The dog is there to eat the steak. [*adapted from F. P. Stieff*]

dawn (n.) a term for the early morning used by people who don't have to get up. [*Oliver Herford*]

death (n.) going over to the majority. [*Thomas Carlyle*]

debate (n.) your side, his side and to hell with it. [*anon.*]

debauchee (n.) (French) someone who has so earnestly pursued pleasure that he has had the misfortune to overtake it. [*Ambrose Bierce*]

decency (n.) shame's conspiracy of silence. [*adapted from George Bernard Shaw*]

deduce (v.) something you get when you squeeze de oranges. [*orig.*]

deficit (n.) what you have when you haven't as much as if you had just nothing. [*anon.*]

degree (n.) what enables a man to get along without use of his intelligence. [*adapted from Alfred Wiggam*]

18

deliberation (n.) the art of examining one's bread to determine which side it is buttered on. [*Ambrose Bierce*]

deluxe (*adj.*) mediocre in a big way. [*L. L. Levinson*]

democracy (n.) a government of bullies tempered by editors. [*R. W. Emerson*]

desertion (n.) a poor man's divorce. [*Arthur Hays*]

desk (n.) a wastebasket with drawers. [*Wall Street Journal*]

destiny (n.) a tyrant's authority for crime and a fool's excuse for failure. [*Ambrose Bierce*]

devil, the (n.) a mixture of a Melbourne taxi driver, a West Australian mining executive, a Queensland policeman, a Sydney lawyer, a Canberra politician and a South Australian. [*orig.*]

diagnosis (n.) a preliminary autopsy. [*anon.*]

diamond (n.) a chunk of coal that stuck to the job. [*B. C. Forbes*]

dictatorship (n.) a government under which everything that is not prohibited is compulsory. [*adapted from Sergei Arutunoff*]

diehard (n.) a man who worships the very ground his head's buried in. [*Bill Stern*]

dignity (n.) window-dressing for a vacant store. [*L. L. Levinson*]

diplomacy (n.) the art of saying "nice doggie" till you can find a rock. [*Wyn Catlin*]

diplomat (n.) a person who can be disarming even though his country isn't. [*Sidney Brody*]

disarmament (n.) an agreement between nations to scuttle all weapons that are obsolete. [*L. L. Levinson*]

discovery (n.) when our wits catch up with nature. [*orig.*]

discretion (n.) putting two and two together and keeping your mouth shut. [*L. L. Levinson*]

disillusion (n.) climbing to the top of the ladder and discovering you have leaned it against the wrong wall. [*orig.*]

distress (n.) a disease incurred by exposure to the prosperity of a friend. [*Ambrose Bierce*]

dividend (n.) a certain per centum per annum perhaps. [*anon.*]

divorce (n.) the sacrament of adultery. [*Jean Guichard*]

divorce lawyer (n.) someone who referees the fight and ends up with the purse. [*anon.*]

doctor (n.) a person upon whom we set our hopes when ill and our dogs when well. [*Ambrose Bierce*]

dog (n.) an intelligent four-footed animal who walks around with some dope on the end of a leash. [*anon.*]

dogma (n.) the collective wisdom of individual ignorance. [*adapted from Thomas Carlyle*]

do-it-yourself (adj.) what you do just before you call in a professional to clean up the mess. [*orig.*]

dollar (n.) a pigeon with a natural homing instinct for the Treasury. [*adapted from Prince Philip*]

doorman (n.) a man who stands out the front of hotels and acts as though he does not know how unimportant you are at home. [*anon.*]

drama (n.) life with the dull bits cut out. [*Alfred Hitchcock*]

drastic (adj.) removing a fly from someone's head with a hatchet. [*orig.*]

dreamer (n.) someone who notices that a rose smells better than a cabbage and concludes that it will also make better soup. [*adapted from H. L. Mencken*]

drunk (adj.) feeling sophisticated but being unable to pronounce it. [*anon.*]

drunkenness (n.) temporary suicide. [*Bertrand Russell*]

dust (n.) mud with the juice squeezed out. [*anon.*]

duty (n.) a stupid man doing something he would otherwise be ashamed of. [*George Bernard Shaw*]

duty-free liquor (n.) flying blind. [*orig.*]

doorman . . . a man who stands out the front of hotels and acts as though he does not know how unimportant you are at home.

eccentric (*adj.*) wearing a hair shirt but being fussy about the cut. [*orig.*]

economist (*n.*) a man who would marry Farrah Fawcett Majors for her money. [*Robert Kolson*]

economy (*n.*) the art of spending money without getting any fun out of it. [*anon.*]

editor (*n.*) a person employed on a newspaper whose business it is to separate the wheat from the chaff and print the chaff. [*Elbert Hubbard*]

education (*n.*) the development of the memory at the expense of the imagination. [*Owen Johnson*]

effigy (*n.*) a scarecrow that does imitations. [*orig.*]

egotism (*n.*) the anaesthetic that dulls the pain of stupidity. [*Frank Leahy*]

egotist (*n.*) a man who thinks if he hadn't been born people would have wondered why. [*Dan Post*]

Eiffel Tower (*n.*) Centrepoint after it has paid back taxes. [*orig.*]

elderly (*adj.*) when you wake up with a hangover and you haven't been out the night before. [*orig.*]

election (*n.*) a method by which the worst possible leader is chosen by the worst possible methods. [*orig.*]

electric chair (*n.*) burning at the stake with all mod. cons. [*L. L. Levinson*]

elephant (n.) an animal with a tail at both ends. [anon.]

embezzler (n.) a thief with an education. [anon.]

emetic (n.) a substance that causes the stomach to take a sudden and enthusiastic interest in outside affairs. [Ambrose Bierce]

engagement (n.) courting disaster. [orig.]

England (n.) the Adelaide of Europe. [orig.]

Englishman (n.) someone who thinks he is moral when he is merely uncomfortable. [George Bernard Shaw]

English novel (n.) a story in which two people fall in love and then complain to each other for 400 pages. [orig.]

ennui (n.) (French) being depressed with a smoking jacket on. [orig.]

enterprise (n.) making toeless shoes a fashion instead of a calamity. [anon.]

enthusiastic (adj.) someone who throws flowers at you. [adapted from Marlene Dietrich]

over enthusiastic (adj.) someone who throws themselves at you. [adapted from Marlene Dietrich]

entrepreneur (n.) (French) a man with a pushcart selling unlaid eggs on consignment after charging the hens for laying them, the customers for buying them and the eggs for being born. [Morton Thompson]

envoy (n.) an honest man sent to lie abroad for his country. [adapted from Sir Henry Wotton]

envy (n.) the mud that failure throws at success. [anon.]

epitaph (n.) a short sarcastic poem. [anon.]

equality (n.) the right of rich and poor, black and white, to bathe in champagne and winter on the Great Barrier Reef. [adapted from Leo Rosten]

erotic (adj.) using a feather as a sex aid. Kinky is when you use the whole duck. [anon.]

eternity (n.) cold storage for high hopes. [adapted from Ambrose Bierce]

ethics (n.) cold feet. [anon.]

etiquette (n.) (French) knowing which fingers to put in your mouth when you whistle for the waiter. [anon.]

evening (n.) the time when people do almost anything to keep from going to bed. [anon.]

everlasting life (n.) the time given to Catholics in which to try and understand the mysteries of their faith. [adapted from Ambrose Bierce]

executive (n.) someone who talks to the visitors while others do the work. [anon.]

existence (n.) creation, recreation, education, procreation, termination, cremation — salvation? [orig.]

expediency (n.) the art of rushing to the defence of the winning side. [Amiel]

political expediency (n.) one eye on the constituency and one eye on the swag. [Mark Twain]

experience (n.) what you have left after you have forgotten her name. [John Barrymore]

expert (n.) an ordinary guy 50 kilometres from home. [anon.]

extremist (n.) someone who leans over backwards to avoid falling flat on his face. [anon.]

eyelids (n.) draperies for the conscience. [Albert Brandt]

fad (n.) something that goes in one era and out the other. [anon.]

fail (v.) the path of least persistence. [anon.]

failure (n.) someone who has blundered but has not cashed in on the experience. [Elbert Hubbard]

faith (n.) throwing your heart over the bar and letting your body follow. [anon.]

fame (n.) a happy combination of talent and timing. [orig.]

fanatic (n.) someone who can't change his mind and won't change the subject. [Winston Churchill]

fanaticism (n.) redoubling your effort when you have forgotten your aim. [George Santayana]

farm (n.) an undeveloped rural site where uncooked meals eat grass. [orig.]

fashion (n.) that by which the fantastic momentarily becomes the universal. [Oscar Wilde]

father (n.) someone who has redeemed the money in his wallet for snapshots. [anon.]

father's day (n.) like mother's day only you don't spend as much. [Mervin Hodas]

faux pas (n.) (French) repartee accidentally entangled with hara kiri. [Jack Goodman]

femme fatale (n.) (French) a dead French woman. [orig.]

fidelity (n.) unadulterated boredom. [Playboy]

finance (n.) the art of passing money from one hand to another until it finally disappears. [L. L. Levinson]

fishing (n.) a delusion surrounded by liars in old clothes. [Don Marquis]

flattery (n.) telling a man what he thinks of himself. [anon.]

flood (n.) a superior degree of dampness. [Ambrose Bierce]

flu (n.) an ill wind that makes everybody blow good. [Lisa Kirk]

flyscreen (n.) a device for keeping insects in the house. [anon.]

foible (n.) a tale or story which generally has a moral, as in Aesop's Foibles. [anon.]

football (n.) running 50 metres to kick a ball behind two goalposts. [orig.]

Association Football (n.) running 50 metres to hit the ball with your head behind two goalposts. [orig.]

Australian Rules Football (n.) running 50 metres to hit the other player in the head from behind and kick the ball behind two goalposts. [orig.]

Rugby League Football (n.) running 50 metres, getting kicked in the behind, ramming the other player's head into the goalposts and sod the ball. [orig.]

forgetfulness (n.) a form of freedom. [Kahlil Gibran]

forgiveness (n.) the fragrance the violet sheds on the heel that has crushed it. [quoted by Mark Twain]

fork (n.) an instrument used for the purpose of putting dead animals in the mouth. [Ambrose Bierce]

founding fathers (n.) dead revolutionaries. [Leo Rosten]

fox hunting (n.) the unspeakable in pursuit of the inedible. [Oscar Wilde]

France (n.) a republic seasoned with garlic. [orig.]

freedom (n.) when one hears the bell at seven in the morning and knows it is the milkman and not the Gestapo. [Georges Bidault]

free press (n.) 100 men imposing their prejudices on 100 million. [Leo Rosten]

free verse (n.) playing tennis with the net down. [Robert Frost]

freeway (n.) a place where drivers under 25 do over 90 and drivers over 90 do under 25. [anon.]

Frenchman (n.) an Italian with a bad temper. [Dennis McEvoy]

French novel (n.) a story in which a man makes beautiful love to a woman for 300 pages and in the last chapter goes home to try and explain it to his wife, who is invariably a dipsomaniac. [orig.]

friend (n.) someone who dislikes the same people you dislike. [adapted from Walter Winchell]

true friend (n.) one who knows all about you and loves you just the same. [orig.]

friendship (n.) the distance between advice and help. [orig.]

frugality (n.) being mean to yourself. [L. L. Levinson]

frustration (n.) when you have ulcers but still aren't successful. [anon.]

fugitive (n.) someone who has the courage to escape his convictions. [anon.]

funeral (n.) a coming out party for a ghost. [L. L. Levinson]

gallows (n.) a human windsock. [orig.]

gambling (n.) getting nothing for something. [Wilson Mizner]

garden (n.) a thing of beauty and a job forever. [anon.]

gender (n.) either masculine or feminine. The masculine is divided into temperate and intemperate and feminine into frigid and torrid. [anon.]

genealogist (n.) someone who traces your family tree as far back as your money will go. [anon.]

general (n.) a man who organises hit jobs for his country, sometimes on a massive scale. [orig.]

General Smuts (n.) what the black races are called in South Africa. [anon.]

genius (n.) a person who shoots at something no-one else can see — and hits it. [anon.]

gentility (n.) what is left over from rich ancestors after the money has gone. [John Ciardi]

gentleman (n.) a guy who would never hit a woman with glasses. [orig.]

German (n.) head man, as in "He's the german of the board." [anon.]

ghetto (n.) a place where any cat with a tail is a tourist. [anon.]

ghost (n.) a shadow of its former self. [L. L. Levinson]

giraffe (n.) a mobile neck. [orig.]

gnu (n.) an animal with a distinctive mating call, giving rise to the expression "Have you heard the gnus today?" [orig.]

goblet (n.) a small male turkey. [anon.]

God (n.) a verb, not a noun. [Richard Fuller]

go-getter (n.) a person who can get both his elbows on both arms of the theatre seat. [anon.]

golden anniversary (n.) a woman's hair net tangled in a man's spectacles at the bottom of a bedpan. [adapted from Don Herold]

golf (n.) a good walk spoiled. [Mark Twain]

gondolier (n.) an infectious disease caused by having sexual relations with Venetian boatmen. [orig.]

Good Friday (n.) the guy who did Robinson Crusoe's housework. [anon.]

good taste (n.) the enemy of creativity. [Picasso]

gorgonzola (n.) the corpse of a dead cheese. [orig.]

gossip (n.) mouth-to-mouth regurgitation. [anon.]

gossip columnist (n.) Judas with a notebook. [orig.]

gourd (n.) a nutritious, energy-filled fruit, as in, "Gourd our strength in ages past." [orig.]

gourmet (n.) a glutton who reads French. [orig.]

government (n.) the art of taking as much money as possible from one class of citizens and giving it to the other. [Voltaire]

grammar (n.) the woman who married grampa. [anon.]

grandfather (n.) a man whose daughter once married someone who was vastly her inferior mentally but consequently gave birth to unbelievably brilliant grandchildren. [anon.]

grandmother (n.) a babysitter who doesn't hang around the refrigerator. [anon.]

gratitude (n.) memory of the heart. [Jean Baptiste Massieu]

greatness (n.) doing something for the first time. [Alexander Smith]

Greek (n.) a Turk pretending to be an Italian. [anon.]

29

Greek tragedy (*n.*) the sort of drama where one character says to another, "If you don't kill mother, I will." [*Spyros Skouras*]

grin (*n.*) a smile that burst. [*adapted from John Donovan*]

grudge (*n.*) the heaviest thing you can carry. [*anon.*]

guillotine (*n.*) a razor that removes all trace of hair from the neck up. [*orig.*]

guts (*n.*) (slang) an infinite capacity for taking life by the scruff of the neck. [*adapted from Christopher Quill*]

Greek tragedy . . . the sort of drama where one character says to another, "If you don't kill mother, I will."

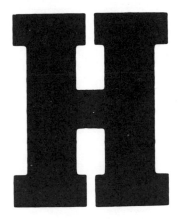

habit (n.) the antidote for desire. [orig.]

hair restorer (n.) balderdash. [orig.]

hand (n.) a singular instrument worn at the end of the human arm and commonly thrust into someone's pocket. [Ambrose Bierce]

handkerchief (n.) a piece of cloth used for treasuring excreta in the pocket. [orig.]

hangover (n.) the wrath of grapes. [Playboy]

happiness (n.) a delicate balance between what one is and what one has. [F. H. Denison]

happy (adj.) having a scratch for every itch. [Ogden Nash]

hard work (n.) an accumulation of easy things that should have been done last week. [anon.]

harlot (n.) a girl who has been tried in the field and found wanton. [orig.]

harp (n.) a nude piano. [Tom Horgan]

haute cuisine (n.) (French) a revolving restaurant. [orig.]

hay fever (n.) flower power. [L. L. Levinson]

heaven (n.) the place where the donkey catches up with the carrot. [anon.]

Hebrew (adj.) a type of Jewish tea. [orig.]

hedgehog (n.) the cactus of the animal kingdom. [Ambrose Bierce]

helicopter (n.) an eggbeater with ambition. [anon.]

31

hell (n.) a place where the Germans are the police, the Russians are the comedians, the Italians are the defence force, the Indonesians build the houses, the Indians run the railways, the Turks cook the food, the Irish make the laws and the common language is Dutch. [anon.]

helplessness (n.) the feeling you have when you are the owner of a sick goldfish. [Kin Hubbard]

hen (n.) an egg's way of making another egg. [Samuel Butler]

heredity (n.) what a man believes in until his son begins to behave like a delinquent. [anon.]

heretic (n.) someone who disagrees with you regarding something neither of you knows anything about. [William Brann]

hero (n.) a man who has behaved as if he was immortal just before he died. [anon.]

highbrow (n.) the kind of person who looks at a sausage and thinks of Picasso. [A. P. Herbert]

high society (n.) the bores and the bored. [Lord Byron]

hire purchase (n.) a method devised to make the months seem shorter. [anon.]

historian (n.) someone who stands at the back of the bus and explains the scenery. [orig.]

history (n.) something that may not have happened, written by someone who was not there and read in schools by people who are not interested. [orig.]

holding company (n.) when you hand an accomplice the goods while a policeman searches you. [Will Rogers]

hole (n.) the nothing that you can break your leg in. [Austin O'Malley]

Holland (n.) the kingdom of the dammed. [orig.]

Hollywood (n.) a place where the stars employ doubles to do all their dangerous jobs for them, excepting marriage. [Tom Jenk]

home (n.) a place where you can scratch any place you itch. [Henry Ainsley]

homo sapiens (n.) (Latin) the only animal that can remain on friendly terms with the victims he intends to eat until he eats them. [Samuel Butler]

honesty (n.) what you will do if you have a guarantee that you will never be found out. [Lord Macaulay]

horizon (n.) a line where the earth and the sky meet, but which disappears when you get there. [anon.]

hors de combat (adj.) (French) a war horse. [anon.]

hors d'oeuvre (n.) (French) a cheese cracker and an anchovy, cut into 20 pieces. [adapted from Jack Benny]

horse sense (n.) rare intelligence that keeps horses from betting on human beings. [Bob Burns]

hospital bed (n.) a parked taxi with the meter running. [Frank Scully]

hospital ward (n.) a place where friends of the patient go to meet other friends of the patient. [Francis Walsh]

house (n.) a place where part of the family waits until the others are through with the car. [anon.]

house warming (n.) the last call for wedding presents. [June Provines]

human being (n.) an ape with possibilities. [adapted from Roy Chapman Andrews]

human nature (n.) when three astronauts go up in a spaceship and there is an argument about who sits by the window. [orig.]

humiliation (n.) the realisation that we have suddenly shrivelled up to our normal dimensions. [Benjamin de Casseres]

hunch (n.) an idea you're afraid is wrong. [Carter Dickson]

hunting (n.) killing time with a shotgun. [orig.]

hurry (n.) a visible form of worry. [Arnold Glasgow]

husband (n.) what is left of the lover after the nerve has been extracted. [Helen Rowland]

hen-pecked husband (n.) someone who has several small mouths to feed and one big one to listen to. [Vince Montemora]

suburban husband (n.) a gardener with sex privileges. [Playboy]

hussy (n.) someone who bares false bosoms against her neighbour. [L. L. Levinson]

hymen (n.) the Greek god of trouble. [orig.]

hypochondriac (*n.*) someone who remembers how many measles he had. [*orig.*]

hypocrisy (*n.*) homage that vice pays to virtue. [*proverb*]

hypocrite (*n.*) a person who has an ace up his sleeve and says that God put it there. [*adapted from Henri Labouchere*]

imagination . . . what sits up with a woman when her husband is late home at night.

iceberg (n.) a permanent wave. [*Mickey Mouse*]

icon (n.) what you fatten pigs with under oak trees. [*anon.*]

idealism (n.) something which tends to increase in direct proportion to one's distance from the problem. [*John Galsworthy*]

idealist (n.) a man with both feet planted firmly in the air. [*Franklin D. Roosevelt*]

ignoramus (n.) someone who doesn't know something you learned yesterday. [*anon.*]

ignorance (n.) what everybody has, only in different subjects. [*Will Rogers*]

imagination (n.) what sits up with a woman when her husband is late home at night. [*anon.*]

immorality (n.) the morality of those who are having a better time. [*H. L. Mencken*]

immortality (n.) a rainy Sunday afternoon with Jerry Lewis re-runs on all three channels. [*orig.*]

impaled (adj.) getting the wrong end of the stick. [*orig.*]

impartial (n.) someone who has nothing to gain from siding with either party in a conflict. [*adapted from Ambrose Bierce*]

impatience (n.) waiting in a hurry. [*anon.*]

impetuous (*adj.*) saying what you think without thinking. [*orig.*]

importance (*n.*) receiving a telegram of more than 10 words. [*adapted from George Ade*]

impresario (*n.*) a promoter with a cape. [*L. L. Levinson*]

incentive (*n.*) the possibility of getting more money than you can earn. [*L. L. Levinson*]

income tax assessor (*n.*) a person who follows you into a revolving door but comes out ahead of you. [*orig.*]

incompatible (*adj.*) two people with a taste for domination. [*adapted from Ambrose Bierce*]

incompetence (*n.*) a one-ulcer man holding down a two-ulcer job. [*Prince Philip*]

individualist (*n.*) a man who lives in the city and commutes to the suburbs. [*Playboy*]

infant (*n.*) an angel whose wings get smaller as its legs get taller. [*anon.*]

inferiority complex (*n.*) what someone has if he has never been to Italy. [*adapted from Samuel Johnson*]

inflation (*n.*) when your son's take-home pay from his first job is more than you paid for the house. [*orig.*]

insane (*adj.*) affected with a high degree of intellectual independence. [*Ambrose Bierce*]

insomnia (*n.*) lying awake all night for an hour. [*Paul Gilbert*]

insurance (*n.*) paying for catastrophe by instalment. [*L. L. Levinson*]

integrity (*n.*) a lofty attitude assumed by someone who is unemployed. [*Oscar Levant*]

intellectual (*n.*) a person educated beyond his intelligence. [*Brandon Matthews*]

intelligence (*n.*) the thing that enables a man to get along without an education. [*Alfred Wiggam*]

interior decorator (*n.*) a person who gets paid for playing practical jokes on other people's homes. [*orig.*]

intuition (*n.*) an uncanny second sense that tells people they are right whether they are or not. [*adapted from Harlan Miller*]

Iran (*n.*) the Middle Ages of the Middle East. [*orig.*]

iris (n.) the part of the eye that smiles, as in "When iris eyes are smiling." [anon.]

Irishman (n.) a simple machine for converting Guinness into urine. [anon.]

Italian (n.) a perambulatory mechanism for converting pastrami into body hair. [orig.]

jealousy (n.) the friendship one woman has for another. [anon.]

jelly (n.) a food found on ice-cream, children and armchairs. [orig.]

jewellery (n.) something people use in order to make out that they're better than other people. [Hugh Roy Cullen]

Jewish novel (n.) a story in which boy meets girl, boy gets girl and then worries what his mother will say. [orig.]

Joan of Arc (n.) Noah's wife. [anon.]

journalism (n.) the arts babblative and scribblative. [Robert Southey]

investigative journalism (n.) putting a well-known figure on a spit and getting the public to turn him. [adapted from George Bernard Shaw]

judge (n.) someone with a sense of justice, a rational mind and an incredible bladder. [adapted from L. C. Payne]

judo (n.) the handshake that bites back. [orig.]

junk (n.) something you throw away just before you need it. [anon.]

jury (n.) twelve persons chosen to decide who has the best lawyer. [Robert Frost]

justice (n.) what we get when the decision is in our favour. [anon.]

kangaroo (*n.*) a pogo stick with a pouch. [*anon.*]

kilt (*n.*) an article of dress first worn by a Scotsman who won a dress in a raffle. [*L. L. Levinson*]

kindergarten teacher (*n.*) a disillusioned girl who used to think she liked children. [*Anna Herbert*]

king (*n.*) someone who reigns over the just and the unjust. [*anon.*]

kiss (*n.*) a vigorous exchange of saliva. [*V. Velsor*]

kleptomaniac (*n.*) a person who helps himself because he can't help himself. [*Henry Morgan*]

knitting (*n.*) an activity that gives women something to think about while they are talking. [*anon.*]

lady (*n.*) a woman who never shows her underwear unintentionally. [*Lillian Day*]

lake (*n.*) a damp place where birds fly around uncooked. [*Joseph Wood Krutch*]

laughter (*n.*) the sun that drives winter from the human face. [*Victor Hugo*]

lawyer (*n.*) someone who rescues your money from your enemies and keeps it himself. [*Lord Brougham*]

laziness (*n.*) the love of physical calm. [*anon.*]

lecture (*n.*) a process by which a professor's notes are passed to his students without necessarily passing through the brains of either. [*Professor R. Stanford*]

legend (*n.*) gossip that has attained the dignity of age. [*adapted from Harry Oliver*]

leisure (*n.*) the mother of philosophy. [*Thomas Hobbes*]

liberal (*n.*) a man with his mind open at both ends. [*anon.*]

liberty (*n.*) the one thing you cannot have unless you are willing to give it to others. [*W. A. White*]

lieutenant commander (*n.*) a lieutenant's wife. [*anon.*]

life (*n.*) playing a violin in public and learning the instrument as you go along. [*Lord Bulwer-Lytton*]

lifetime (*n.*) a predicament that precedes death. [*Henry James*]

lipstick (n.) a device to make every kiss tell. [L. L. Levinson]

lisp (n.) to call a spade a thpade. [Oliver Herford]

literature (n.) the orchestration of platitudes. [Thornton Wilder]

litigate (v.) what an Italian has in front of his little house. [orig.]

logic (n.) going wrong with confidence. [J. W. Krutch]

loneliness (n.) the feeling you have when you are without money among relatives. [anon.]

long-service leave (n.) an abscess in recess. [orig.]

loser (n.) an innocent bystander who gets killed after a battle by an unexploded shell and then has his name spelled wrongly in the newspapers. [orig.]

born loser (n.) a virgin with syphilis. [orig.]

love (n.) the distant chord of a violin and the triumphant twang of a bed spring. [adapted from S. J. Perelman]

love affair (n.) a season pass on the shuttle between heaven and hell. [anon.]

lover (n.) someone who tries to be more amiable than it is possible for him to be. [anon.]

Luther, Martin (n.) a religious fanatic who died a horrible death. He was excommunicated by a bull. [anon.]

machinery (n.) the subconscious mind of the world. [*Gerald Stanley Lee*]

madman (n.) a clique of one. [*adapted from George Bernard Shaw*]

magistrate (n.) someone who has risen by his gravity. [*adapted from Sydney Smith*]

Mahatma Gandhi (n.) the spiritual leader of India who won his nation independence. He rose from humble beginnings as a cloakroom attendant, when he was known as Mahatma Coat. [*orig.*]

majority (n.) a few powerful leaders, a certain number of accommodating rogues and subservient weaklings and a mass of men who trudge after them without in the least knowing their own minds. [*Goethe*]

male menopause (n.) the time when a man starts turning off the lights for economical rather than romantic reasons. [*adapted from John Merino*]

malice (n.) the reaction caused by the addition of human nature to a motor car. [*orig.*]

man (n.) an ingenious assembly of portable plumbing. [*Christopher Morley*]

management (n.) an organisation that makes it difficult for other people to work. [*Peter Drucker*]

managing director (n.) someone who is known by the company he keeps. [*anon.*]

manic depressive (n.) a person who is never happy unless he is miserable, and even then he is worried that he may be happy tomorrow, and this makes him insecure. [orig.]

manners (n.) the noise you don't make eating soup. [L. L. Levinson]

marital bliss (n.) the peace of the double bed after the rigours of the drive-in. [adapted from Mrs P. Cambell]

market (n.) three women and a goose. [Italian proverb]

market analyst (n.) a weather forecaster who sends other people broke instead of getting them wet. [orig.]

marriage (n.) the effort a man makes to be satisfied with only one woman. [Paul Géraldy]

martyr (n.) a pile of wood set on fire with a man on top. [anon.]

martyrdom (n.) the only way in which a man can become famous without ability. [George Bernard Shaw]

materialism (n.) collateral thinking. [orig.]

mathematician (n.) someone who is able to count up to 20 without taking off his shoes. [Mickey Mouse]

matrimony (n.) a device for getting people better acquainted with themselves. [orig.]

mauve (n.) pink trying to be purple. [James Whistler]

mealtime (n.) the only time a child won't eat. [orig.]

mechanic (n.) a person who picks your pocket from underneath your car. [orig.]

medical practitioner (n.) someone who pillages his triumphs and buries his mistakes. [orig.]

medicine (n.) a drug that is currently on the market and has to date no known dangerous side effects. [orig.]

mediocre (adj.) wanting to be degenerate and not quite making it. [adapted from George Ade]

mediocrity (n.) the rugged will to lose. [orig.]

meek (adj.) a man who soothes a tiger by allowing himself to be eaten. [Konrad Adenauer]

melancholy (n.) the pleasure of being sad. [Victor Hugo]

member of parliament (n.) a $12,000-a-year man trying to hang on to a $35,000-a-year job. [adapted from Clinton Gilbert]

memoirs (n.) the back fence of history. [adapted from George Meredith]

memory (n.) what tells a man his wife's birthday was yesterday. [Mario Rocco]

menagerie (n.) a prison for animals. [orig.]

menopause (n.) when a woman is too young to join a bowling club and too old to rush up to the net. [adapted from F. P. Adams]

mermaid (n.) part virgin, part sturgeon. [anon.]

microbe (n.) a bug's bug. [orig.]

middle age (n.) when you are sitting at home on a Saturday night and the telephone rings and you hope it isn't for you. [Ogden Nash]

middle class (n.) the art of wearing last year's suit, driving this year's car and living on next year's income. [anon.]

Middle East (n.) a region where oil is thicker than blood. [James Holland]

millennium (n.) something like a centennial only it has more legs. [anon.]

mine (n.) a hole in the ground owned by a liar. [Mark Twain]

minister (n.) an agent of a higher power with a lower responsibility. [Ambrose Bierce]

miser (n.) someone whose fortune has acquired him. [Bion]

missionary (n.) someone who makes a place safe for hypocrisy. [adapted from Thomas Wolfe]

missionary in Borneo (n.) God's gift to the starving. [adapted from Oscar Wilde]

mistress (n.) something that goes between a mister and a mattress. [Joe Lewis]

mixed emotions (n.) watching your mother-in-law drive over a cliff in your new Ferrari. [Long John Lebel]

mob (n.) five or more men, three or more women, one or more children. [orig.]

model driver (n.) someone who just saw the guy ahead of him get a traffic ticket. [anon.]

moderate (n.) a prude after a big dinner. [orig.]

modern art (n.) what happens when painters stop looking at girls and persuade themselves that they have a better idea. [*John Ciardi*]

modern warfare (n.) the application of the mechanics of force to human nature. [*General Douglas MacArthur*]

modesty (n.) a bait angled for praise. [*G. K. Chesterton*]

money (n.) a more pleasant alternative to good advice. [*orig.*]

monkey (n.) God's sarcasm on the human race. [*adapted from H. W. Beecher*]

moonlighter (n.) someone who holds down two jobs so that he can drive from one to the other in a better car. [*anon.*]

moral indignation (n.) jealousy with a halo. [*H. G. Wells*]

moralist (n.) someone who is so full of principles there is no room left for either tolerance or compassion. [*adapted from Lord Moran*]

morals (n.) what you have before someone discovers the truth about you. [*orig.*]

Mormon (n.) an American expatriate with four wives and one bicycle. [*orig.*]

mortuary (n.) a place where the dead are laid to await the final coming of the medical student. [*adapted from Ambrose Bierce*]

moth (n.) a butterfly that eats holes. [*orig.*]

motherhood (n.) feeding the mouth that bites you. [*Peter de Vries*]

mountain range (n.) a cooking stove used at high altitudes. [*anon.*]

mushrooms (n.) vegetables which, because they grow in damp places, always look like umbrellas. [*anon.*]

musical (n.) disorderly conduct occasionally interrupted by talk. [*George Ade*]

music lover (n.) a man who, on hearing a soprano in the bathroom, puts his ear to the keyhole. [*Kalends*]

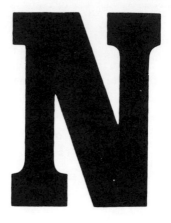

naive (*adj.*) trying to leap a chasm in two jumps. [*orig.*]

narcissism (*n.*) walking down Lover's Lane and holding your own hand. [*adapted from Fred Allen*]

nation (*n.*) a society united by delusion about its ancestry and by a common hatred of its neighbours. [*W. R. Inge*]

nationalist (*n.*) a man controlled by geography. [*George Santayana*]

nature (*n.*) the verb "to eat" in the active and the passive. [*W. R. Inge*]

net (*n.*) holes surrounded by pieces of string. [*anon.*]

neurotic (*adj.*) when you worry about things that didn't happen in the past, instead of worrying about something that won't happen in the future, like normal people. [*anon.*]

neutral (*adj.*) someone who, at a time of great moral crisis, decides not to make a decision. [*orig.*]

news (*n.*) the same thing happening every day, only to different people. [*anon.*]

newspaper (*n.*) a portable screen behind which a man can hide from an old lady standing up on a bus. [*anon.*]

New York (*n.*) Noisyville-on-the-Subway. [*O. Henry*]

New Zealand (*n.*) the semicolon of the South Pacific. [*orig.*]

Niagara Falls (n.) water on the rocks. [*L. L. Levinson*]

nobility (n.) that strata of society which consumes without producing. [*adapted from George Bernard Shaw*]

noise (n.) a stench in the ear. [*Ambrose Bierce*]

nonentity (n.) someone who goes to his own funeral and is made to stand at the back by the usher. [*orig.*]

nose (n.) the extreme outpost of the face. [*Ambrose Bierce*]

nostalgia (n.) recalling the fun without remembering the pain. [*unknown*]

novel (n.) a book that has a blonde on the jacket and no jacket on the blonde. [*Earl Wilson*]

Nullarbor (n.) the same kilometre 700 times. [*orig.*]

nonentity . . . someone who goes to his own funeral and is made to stand at the back by the usher.

47

obituary (*n.*) a belated advertisement for a line of goods that has been permanently discontinued. [*Irvin Cobb*]

objective (*adj.*) being rational when you have nothing to lose. [*orig.*]

oblivion (*n.*) life's dumping ground. [*adapted from Ambrose Bierce*]

obstacle (*n.*) a difficulty you see when you take your eyes off the goal. [*anon.*]

occupational therapy (*n.*) amusing the patient while nature cures the disease. [*adapted from Voltaire*]

ocean (*n.*) a large body of water entirely surrounded by trouble. [*anon.*]

office manager (*n.*) a clerk who has a partition round his desk. [*orig.*]

old age (*n.*) when things begin to wear out, fall out and spread out. [*adapted from Beryl Pfizer*]

opera (*n.*) when a guy gets stabbed in the back and, instead of bleeding, he sings. [*Ed Gardner*]

opinion (*n.*) the arrangement of prejudices. [*orig.*]

opium (*n.*) the far out of the Far East. [*orig.*]

opportunism (*n.*) getting a tan by basking in reflected glory. [*orig.*]

opportunist (*n.*) a man who offers his seat to a lady as he is about to get off the bus. [*orig.*]

oppressor (*n.*) a martyr who is returned to power. [*orig.*]

optimism (*n.*) looking for lodgings with a violin under one arm and a trombone under the other. [*anon.*]

optimist (*n.*) a cheerful guy who is blissfully unaware of what is going to happen to him. [*anon.*]

oratory (*n.*) the art of making deep noises from the chest sound like important messages from the brain. [*H. I. Phillips*]

Orient (*n.*) the Far East. In Perth, it's Sydney. [*orig.*]

originality (*n.*) undetected plagiarism. [*W. R. Inge*]

Oslo (*n.*) the biggest village in Norway. [*anon.*]

DO NOT SKATEBOARD IN EMTY POOL

optimist . . . a cheerful guy who is blissfully unaware of what is going to happen to him.

painting (*n.*) the art of protecting flat surfaces from the weather and exposing them to the critics. [*Ambrose Bierce*]

papal bull (*n.*) a cow that was kept at the Vatican to supply milk for the Pope's children. [*anon.*]

paradise (*n.*) the Luna Park of Limbo Land. [*orig.*]

paradox (*n.*) truth standing on its head to attract attention. [*Richard le Gallienne*]

paraffin (*n.*) the next order of angels above the seraphim. [*anon.*]

paratrooper (*n.*) a soldier who climbs down trees he never climbed up. [*anon.*]

parents (*n.*) people who use the rhythm method of birth control. [*Mary Fink*]

parking space (*n.*) an unoccupied area on the other side of the street. [*Mac Benoff*]

parliament (*n.*) where a man gets up to speak, says nothing, nobody listens — and then everyone disagrees. [*anon.*]

parrot (*n.*) the only creature gifted with the power of speech that is content to repeat what it hears without trying to make a good story out of it. [*anon.*]

party (*n.*) a gathering held to enable 40 people to talk about themselves at the same time. The man who remains after the liquor is gone is the host. [*Fred Allen*]

pas de deux (*n.*) (French) the father of twins. [*anon.*]

passengers (n.) shock absorbers on buses. [anon.]

passion (n.) the wine of existence. [adapted from H. W. Beecher]

passport (n.) a photograph that a man laughs at without realising that this is the way his friends see him. [Boston Herald]

pastoralist (n.) a farmer who owns a station wagon. [anon.]

patience (n.) a minor form of despair, disguised as a virtue. [Ambrose Bierce]

patriotism (n.) the conviction that your country is superior to all other countries because you were born in it. [George Bernard Shaw]

patron (n.) a customer who doesn't ask prices. [L. L. Levinson]

pawnbroker (n.) someone who lives off the flat of the land. [Lionel Shelley]

peace treaty (n.) an agreement setting forth the basis for the next war. [L. L. Levinson]

pear (n.) an apple with its girdle off. [Charlie McCarthy]

pearl (n.) an oyster tumour. [orig.]

pedestrian (n.) there are two types: the quick and the dead. [anon.]

penal code (n.) a system of revenge whereby the state attempts to imitate the criminal. [Elbert Hubbard]

penthouse (n.) a retreat where you make advances. [Playboy]

perfectionist (n.) a person, who, on getting to heaven, finds he doesn't like God. [orig.]

period (n.) a dot at the end of a sentence. Period costumes are dresses covered with dots. [anon.]

permanent wave (n.) a kink for a day. [anon.]

perseverance (n.) obstinacy for a good cause. [Laurence Sterne]

persuasion (n.) operating on a donkey at both ends, with a carrot and a stick. [adapted from Winston Churchill]

pessimism (n.) when, having the choice of two evils, you choose both. [anon.]

pessimist (n.) a man who, when he smells flowers, looks around for the coffin. [adapted from H. L. Mencken]

pharmacist (*n.*) a person in a white coat who stands behind a cosmetic counter selling five-dollar watches. [*anon.*]

philanthropist (*n.*) someone who gives away what he should give back. [*anon.*]

philistine (*n.*) someone who thinks that Paderewski is a racehorse. [*orig.*]

philosopher (*n.*) a blind person in a dark room looking for a black hat that is not there. [*anon.*]

philosophy (*n.*) masturbation of the mind. [*orig.*]

piccolo (*n.*) the smallest instrument a musician can play in public and still maintain his self respect. [*anon.*]

pier (*n.*) a disappointed bridge. [*James Joyce*]

piety (*n.*) a good time, as in "Come on over Saturday night, we're having a piety." [*orig.*]

pig (*n.*) an animal that has four legs and flies. [*adapted from Fred Allen*]

pilgrim (*n.*) a traveller who goes abroad to pray in famous churches, as opposed to a tourist, who travels abroad to take photographs of them. [*orig.*]

pious (*adj.*) when someone reads from the Bible as if he is the author. [*orig.*]

piracy (*n.*) commerce without manners. [*L. L. Levinson*]

platform (*n.*) an arena in which a politician wrestles with his record at election time. [*orig.*]

platonic (*adj.*) sex above the ears. [*adapted from Thyra Winslow*]

platonic love (*n.*) the gun that makes out it isn't loaded. [*anon.*]

playboy (*n.*) a man who comes to work from a different direction every morning. [*L. L. Levinson*]

plumber (*n.*) someone who gets paid for sleeping under other people's sinks. [*anon.*]

Pluto (*n.*) the farthest dog from earth. [*orig.*]

poetic justice (*n.*) when your dentist tells you it isn't going to hurt and then catches his hand in the drill. [*orig.*]

poetry (n.) what Milton saw when he went blind. [Don Marquis]

poise (n.) raising one's eyebrow instead of the roof. [Howard Newton]

poker (n.) a game in which a good deal depends upon a good deal. [anon.]

Poland (n.) a place where, if Bo Derek should walk along the street in nothing but shoes, people would look at her shoes first. [adapted from John Gunther]

politeness (n.) a pleasing way to get nowhere with women. [anon.]

political campaign (n.) an emotional orgy designed to distract attention from the real issues. [James H. Robinson]

political candidate (n.) an orang-utan trying to play the violin. [adapted from Honoré de Balzac]

politician (n.) an arse upon which everyone has sat except a man. [e. e. cummings]

politics (n.) the art of obtaining money from the rich and votes from the poor, on the pretext of protecting each from the other. [Oscar Ameringer]

pollution (n.) Mother Nature going prematurely grey. [adapted from I. Kupcinet]

polygon (n.) a dead parrot. [anon.]

pompous (adj.) having stuffing instead of guts. [adapted from L. L. Levinson]

poodle (n.) a cross between a hamster and a tea cosy. [orig.]

toy poodle (n.) a rat with a perm. [orig.]

poseur (n.) (French) someone with just enough learning to misquote. [orig.]

positive (adj.) being mistaken at the top of your voice. [Ambrose Bierce]

possibly (adv.) no in three syllables. [L. L. Levinson]

posterity (n.) the patriotic name for grandchildren. [Art Linkletter]

potato (n.) an Irish avocado. [Fred Allen]

poverty (n.) the lack of much. [Antipater of Macedonia]

prayer (n.) a little message to God, sent at night to get the cheaper rate. [anon.]

pregnant (adj.) the past tense of virgin. [anon.]

prejudice (n.) a device enabling you to form opinions without getting the facts. [Robert Quiller]

premier (n.) a personage attached to a state to prevent it from going ahead too fast. [anon.]

premiere (n.) a large number of people standing around looking famous. [Denis Mackail]

pretension (n.) the art of plunging into a sea of platitudes, and swimming confidently towards the white cliffs of conceit. [adapted from W. Somerset Maugham]

priest (n.) in Australia, the third person of the Holy Trinity, the mother and the doctor being the other two. [orig.]

prime minister (n.) the arch mediocrity. [adapted from Benjamin Disraeli]

prince (n.) a young gentleman who, in romance, bestows his affections on a peasant girl and, in real life, on his best friends' wives. [Ambrose Bierce]

princess (n.) an accident that occurred in the attempt to create a prince. [Manfred Gottfried]

principles (n.) prejudice, whitewashed and surmounted by a neon halo. [anon.]

prisoner (n.) a criminal who is so stupid that even the police can catch him. [orig.]

P. R. man (n.) a press agent with a manicure. [Alan Gordon]

procrastinator (n.) someone who puts off till tomorrow the things he's already put off till today. [anon.]

professor (n.) someone whose job it is to tell students how to solve the problems of life which he himself tried to avoid by becoming a professor. [anon.]

profound (adj.) when he who hears doesn't know what he who speaks means, and when he who speaks doesn't know what he himself means. [adapted from Voltaire]

progress (n.) when it takes less time to fly across the Atlantic than it does to drive to the office. [anon.]

projectile (n.) the final arbiter in international disputes. [Ambrose Bierce]

promoter (n.) someone who will furnish the ocean if you will furnish the ship. [anon.]

prophet (n.) a person who says "I told you so" to posterity. [orig.]

prudish (adj.) being ashamed to say what you are not ashamed to think. [orig.]

psychiatrist (n.) a person who owns a couch and charges you for lying on it. [Edwin Brock]

psychiatry (n.) spending $50 an hour to squeal on your mother. [Mike Connoly]

psychoanalysis (n.) the disease it purports to cure. [Karl Kraus]

psychologist (n.) a man who, when a good-looking girl enters the room, looks at everyone else. [anon.]

psychopath (n.) someone who lives in an ivory tower and dribbles over the battlements. [orig.]

puberty (n.) the awkward age when a child is too old to say something cute and too young to say something sensible. [anon.]

public office (n.) the last refuge of the incompetent. [Boies Penrose]

public servant (n.) a sort of fungus that attaches itself to a desk. [Fred Allen]

public service (n.) ten men doing the work of one. [anon.]

publishing (n.) the art of buying paper and selling it again at a profit. [adapted from Charles Dana]

punctuality (n.) the art of guessing how late the other person is going to be. [anon.]

punter (n.) a guy who buys $200 worth of hope for two minutes for two dollars. [adapted from Eddy Howard]

purgatory (n.) Adelaide on Sunday. [orig.]

puritan (n.) someone who hates bull fighting not because it gives pain to the bull, but because it gives pleasure to the spectators. [Thomas Macaulay]

puritanism (n.) the haunting fear that someone, somewhere, may be happy. [H. L. Mencken]

put (v.) placing something where you want it. [anon.]

putt (v.) being unable to place something where you want it. [anon.]

pyramids (n.) the range of mountains between France and Spain. [anon.]

quark (*n.*) the sound made by an English duck. [*orig.*]

quarrel (*n.*) two people trying to make each other see reason. [*orig.*]

Queen (*n.*) Britain's landlady. [*orig.*]

queer (*n.*) a man who prefers boys to girls. An Australian queer is a man who prefers girls to beer. [*anon.*]

rack (n.) a device for stretching out the truth. [orig.]

radicals (n.) those who advance to consolidate a position for conservatives to occupy in 100 years time. [anon.]

rage (n.) a mighty wind which blows out the lamp of the mind. [adapted from Robert Ingersoll]

rape (n.) rapid intention without lengthy deception. [orig.]

rationale (n.) the use of intelligence to avoid the truth. [anon.]

realist (n.) a man about to do something he is ashamed of. [adapted from Sydney Harris]

reason (n.) an instrument for bolstering up prejudices. [Elbert Hubbard]

reckless driver (n.) someone who overtakes you despite all your efforts to stop him. [Lincoln Parker]

red-light district (n.) an erogenous zone. [Playboy]

refinance (v.) a debt warmed up. [Len Elliot]

refinement (n.) the ability to yawn without opening your mouth. [anon.]

reformer (n.) someone who looks down his nose for a living. [orig.]

refugees (n.) people who vote with their feet. [anon.]

reindeer (n.) a horse with a hatrack. [anon.]

relations (n.) a tedious pack of people who haven't the remotest knowledge of how to live or the slightest instinct about when to die. [Oscar Wilde]

religion (n.) a broad concept trapped in narrow minds. [orig.]

remarry (v.) the triumph of hope over experience. [Samuel Johnson]

repartee (n.) a duel fought with the points of jokes. [Max Eastman]

reprobate (n.) someone who has sold his soul to the devil and now lives with a good conscience on the proceeds. [orig.]

republic (n.) the art of running the circus from the monkey cage. [adapted from H. L. Mencken]

reputation (n.) what people say about you behind your back. [orig.]

resignation (n.) the past tense of investigation. [orig]

resort (n.) a place where the natives live on your vacation till next summer. [anon.]

responsibility (n.) something we look forward to with distaste, fulfil with reluctance when we have it and then boast about endlessly afterwards. [anon.]

reunion (n.) a meeting where your old classmates are so grey and wrinkled and bald that they don't recognise you. [adapted from Bennett Cerf]

revolution (n.) shifting the boot of tyranny to another foot. [orig.]

rhubarb (n.) bloodshot celery. [anon.]

rice paddy (n.) a type of Irish curry. [orig.]

riches (n.) the savings of many in the hands of one. [Eugene Debs]

riding (n.) the art of keeping a horse between yourself and the ground. [London Times]

rigor mortis (n.) (Latin) nature's way of telling us to slow down. [Newsweek]

riots (n.) the language of the unheard. [Martin Luther King]

river (n.) water under the bridge. [orig.]

road house (n.) a place where you fill the car and drain the family. [*Clyde Moore*]

road map (n.) a large piece of paper that tells you everything you need to know except how to fold it up again. [*anon.*]

Romeo (n.) someone who ends all his sentences with a proposition. [*orig.*]

Royal Mint (n.) what the Queen grows in her garden. [*anon.*]

R.S.P.C.A. (n.) organisation devoted to letting the cat out of the bag. [*orig.*]

rudeness (n.) a weak man's imitation of strength. [*Eric Hoffer*]

rumba (n.) waving goodbye without using your hands. [*anon.*]

rumour (n.) a baby myth. [*orig.*]

Russia (n.) the bastard child of Karl Marx and Catherine the Great. [*Lord Atlee*]

Russian novel (n.) a story in which the main character sulks for 600 pages. [*orig.*]

rut (n.) a shallow grave. [*anon.*]

sacrifice (*n.*) a form of bargaining. [*Holbrook Jackson*]

sadist (*n.*) someone who is kind to masochists. [*Vincent McHugh*]

saint (*n.*) someone who is hell to live with. [*R. C. Cushing*]

salesman (*n.*) a fellow who chats pleasantly while he overcharges you. [*adapted from Kin Hubbard*]

sales manager (*n.*) a manic depressive on the upswing. [*adapted from Archie Mayo*]

salesmanship (*n.*) the difference between rape and ecstasy. [*Lord Thompson of Fleet*]

sales resistance (*n.*) the triumph of mind over patter. [*anon.*]

sarcasm (*n.*) striking while the irony is hot. [*adapted from Don Quinn*]

savings (*n.*) money that sleeps while you work. [*L. L. Levinson*]

savoir-faire (*n.*) (French) knowing which fork to pick your nose with at a dinner party. [*orig.*]

scandal (*n.*) something that has to be bad to be good. [*anon.*]

sceptic (*n.*) someone who once lost his wallet in a church while standing between a policeman and a nun. [*orig.*]

scholar (*n.*) someone who so overflows with learning that he is standing in the slops. [*orig.*]

school (n.) a place where dust is shaken out of a book into an empty skull. [*adapted from Ambrose Bierce*]

schooling (n.) the process of casting false pearls before real swine. [*Professor Irwin Edman*]

science (n.) the orderly arrangement of what, at the moment, appear to be facts. [*anon.*]

scientist (n.) someone who prolongs our expectation of life so that we can have the time to pay for the gadgets he invents. [*anon.*]

scoundrel (n.) a man who won't stay bought. [*William Tweed*]

scrooge (n.) a man who lives miserably so he can die rich. [*adapted from Henry Fielding*]

scruples (n.) something that tells you to go ahead and do the right thing after you have considered doing the wrong thing and decided it wasn't worth the risk. [*adapted from L. L. Levinson*]

secret (n.) something you tell just one person at a time. [*anon.*]

seduction (n.) Scotch and sofa. [*Playboy*]

self assurance (n.) the ability to be at ease conspicuously. [*anon.*]

self denial (n.) the effect of prudence on rascality. [*George Bernard Shaw*]

self indulgence (n.) masturbating, and faking the orgasm. [*anon.*]

selfish (n.) devoid of consideration for the selfishness of others. [*Ambrose Bierce*]

self-made man (n.) one who worships his creator. [*William Cowper*]

self-proclaimed Messiah (n.) someone who wears a crown of thorns cocked over one eye. [*orig.*]

self restraint (n.) feeling your oats without sowing them. [*Shannon Fife*]

seminar (n.) a meeting at which people talk about the things they should already be doing. [*anon.*]

senility (n.) any shortcoming belonging to a person over 80. [*orig.*]

sense of humour (n.) lack of sympathy. [*Tony Hancock*]

sermon (*n.*) a long monologue which gives the speaker a chance to tell people where to get off without fear of being insulted back. [*orig.*]

settlement (*n.*) the art of slicing a piece of cake in such a way that everyone believes he has received the biggest piece. [*adapted from Jan Peerce*]

sex (*n.*) the tomato ketchup that the adolescent palate pours on every course in the menu. [*adapted from Mary Day Winn*]

shin (*n.*) a device for finding furniture in the dark. [*anon.*]

shoulder strap (*n.*) a thin strip of material that prevents an attraction from becoming a sensation. [*anon.*]

shrew (*n.*) a woman who darns her husband's socks and socks her darn husband. [*anon.*]

sic transit gloria mundi (Latin) Gloria was sick on the train last Monday. [*orig.*]

sightseer (*n.*) a man who only goes inside a church when he is on holiday. [*orig.*]

silicone (*n.*) a substance for making mountains out of molehills. [*orig.*]

skeleton (*n.*) a leper in a wind tunnel. [*anon.*]

skiing (*n.*) whoosh! then walk a mile. [*anon.*]

slot machine (*n.*) the only thing that can stand with its back to the wall and defy the world. [*Goodman Ace*]

slum (*n.*) the Victorian contribution to architecture. [*Robert Jordan*]

small businessman (*n.*) someone who is willing to sell his products without hiring a researcher to find out why people want them. [*Wall Street Journal*]

smile (*n.*) the shortest distance between two people. [*anon.*]

smirk (*n.*) a thought that appears on the face. [*anon.*]

smog (*n.*) the Air Apparent [*Rod McLean*]

smoking (*n.*) the main cause of statistics. [*Fletcher Knebel*]

smug (*adj.*) adding a column of figures and getting the same total as you did the first time. [*anon.*]

sneer (*n.*) the weapon of the weak. [*James Russell Lowell*]

snob (n.) a man who thinks he sired his own ancestors. [orig.]

snobbery (n.) the Pox Britannica. [Anthony Sampson]

snore (n.) the "Moonlight Sonata" of the nose. [orig.]

social climber (n.) someone who ingratiates himself with Christ so that he can get to know God. [orig.]

social climbing (n.) the art of stepping on the right people. [Earl Wilson]

socialism (n.) a system which is workable only in heaven, where it isn't needed, and in hell, where they've already got it. [Cecil Palmer]

solicitor (n.) someone who is more honourable than a politician but less honourable than a prostitute. [adapted from Alex King]

solvent (adj.) when you don't bother to smooth down your hair before entering your bank. [L. L. Levinson]

sophistication (n.) the art of paying attention without listening. [orig.]

sordid (adj.) lifelike. [L. L. Levinson]

South Australia (n.) an oasis of insignificance sandwiched between two deserts of parochialism. [orig.]

space (n.) the stature of God. [Joseph Joubert]

Spaniard (n.) someone with more christian names than underwear. [orig.]

specialist (n.) a doctor whose patients confine their ailments to office hours. [anon.]

spinster (n.) a woman who knows all the answers but has never been asked the question. [Earlene White]

spite (n.) anger that is afraid to show itself. [anon.]

spitting image (n.) a child being fed cereal by his parents. [Imogene Fey]

spook (n.) something everyone is afraid of and no-one believes in. [orig.]

spoon (n.) a small shovel for the mouth. [L. L. Levinson]

stalactite (n.) a stiff piece of water. [adapted from Fred Allen]

star (*n.*) a person who works hard all his life to become well known and then wears dark glasses to avoid being recognised. [*Fred Allen*]

statesman (*n.*) a dead politician. [*Bob Edwards*]

elder statesman (*n.*) a politician who is politically dead. [*Harry Truman*]

statesmanship (*n.*) formality without morality. [*adapted from Mark Twain*]

statistician (*n.*) someone who can draw a mathematically precise line from an unwarranted assumption to a foregone conclusion. [*anon.*]

status quo (*n.*) (Latin) Latin for "The mess we're in." [*anon.*]

steam (*n.*) water gone crazy with the heat. [*Mickey Mouse*]

steel wool (*n.*) the result of shearing a hydraulic ram. [*anon.*]

stenographer (*n.*) a girl you pay to learn how to spell while she's looking for a husband. [*Franklin Jones*]

stoicism (*n.*) the quality that keeps a woman smiling when a departing guest stands at the open screen door and lets in all the flies. [*anon.*]

storeroom (*n.*) a place to keep all the junk we do not want others to have. [*orig.*]

straitjacket (*n.*) a windcheater with button-down sleeves designed to stop madmen from picking their nose. [*orig.*]

street (*n.*) a broad, flat surface used for the storage of "no parking" signs. [*Wall Street Journal*]

submarine (*n.*) a battleship that dunks. [*anon.*]

subtlety (*n.*) the art of saying what you want to say and getting out of range before it is understood. [*anon.*]

suburb (*n.*) a place where people spend money they don't have, to buy things they don't need, to impress people they don't like. [*adapted from Lewis Henry*]

suburbanite (*n.*) a person who hires someone to cut the grass so he can play golf for the exercise. [*anon.*]

suburbia (n.) the place where, by the time you've finished paying off the mortgage, the suburbs have moved 20 kilometres farther out. [anon.]

subversive (adj.) rocking the boat yourself and telling everyone it's a storm. [orig.]

success (n.) doing what you want to do and making money from it. [anon.]

suicide (n.) belated acquiescence to the opinion of one's wife's relatives. [H. L. Mencken]

Sunday driver (n.) someone who speeds up so he can pass you, then slows down. [anon.]

Sunday drunk (n.) an unmanageable condition of spiritual ecstasy. [anon.]

Sunday school (n.) a prison in which children do penance for the guilty conscience of their parents. [II. L. Mencken]

superiority (n.) the attitude we adopt towards people we personally dislike. [adapted from Oscar Wilde]

superstition (n.) religion without God. [Joseph Hall]

surgeon (n.) a plumber who works standing up. [orig.]

suspicion (n.) the friendship that one actress has for another. [Eleonora Dose]

sweater (n.) a garment a child wears when his mother feels cold. [anon.]

swimming pool (n.) a crowd of people with water in it. [anon.]

sympathy (n.) what one person offers another in exchange for details. [anon.]

suburbanite . . . a person who hires someone to cut the grass so he can play golf for the exercise.

tact (*n.*) closing your mouth before someone tells you to. [*anon.*]

talent (*n.*) the infinite capacity for imitating genius. [*Benjamin de Casseres*]

taste (*n.*) a leaning towards the styles you admire. [*anon.*]

taxation (*n.*) the art of plucking the goose to obtain the largest amount of feathers with the least amount of hissing. [*Jean Baptiste Colbert*]

tax collector (*n.*) a taxidermist who stuffs you and keeps the skin. [*orig.*]

taxes (*n.*) supporting the government in the style to which it has become accustomed. [*adapted from Farmer's Almanac*]

taxpayer (*n.*) the soft cushion on which the public service reposes. [*orig.*]

teacher (*n.*) a person who makes the little things in life count. [*anon.*]

technology (*n.*) what happens when impossibility yields to necessity. [*adapted from Adlai Stevenson*]

teenager (*n.*) someone who is young enough to know everything. [*orig.*]

teetotaller (*n.*) someone who practises moderation to excess. [*orig.*]

television (*n.*) a medium which allows millions of people to listen to the same joke at the same time and still be lonely. [*T. S. Eliot*]

television soapie (n.) chewing gum for the eyes. [adapted from Bertrand Russell]

temperament (n.) temper that is too old to spank. [Charlotte Greenwood]

temptation (n.) an irresistible force at work on a movable body. [H. L. Mencken]

tenacity (n.) biting off more than you can chew — and chewing it. [orig.]

terra firma (n.) (Latin) love of solid ground, literally "The more firma, the less terra." [anon.]

theatre critic (n.) a man who does not see the play because he is too busy watching his reaction. [adapted from E. B. White]

theologian (n.) someone who has dipped in the well of all knowledge and come up dry. [orig.]

theory of relativity (n.) the piece that passeth all understanding. [orig.]

thesis (n.) the transference of bones from one graveyard to another. [J. Frank Dobie]

third world development (n.) a cannibal using a knife and fork. [Stanislaw Lec]

thrift (n.) the most wonderful virtue of any ancestor. [anon.]

thriller (n.) a book you enjoy so much that when you put it down you say, "Thank God that's over." [adapted from Morton Thompson]

throne (n.) a piece of lumber covered with a velvet rug. [Napoleon]

time (n.) nature's way of preventing everything happening at once. [anon.]

timidity (n.) the proudest form of grovelling. [Gustave Flaubert]

tip (n.) a small sum of money you give to someone because you are afraid he wouldn't like not being paid for something you haven't asked him to do. [Ann Caesar]

toastmaster (n.) a person who introduces people who need no introduction. [anon.]

tomorrow (n.) a labour-saving device. [anon.]

tongue (n.) the neck's enemy. [Arabian proverb.]

tonic (n.) something we would complain about if it came out of the tap. [orig.]

tooth fairy (n.) a gay dentist. [orig.]

tourist (*n.*) someone who travels to see things that are different and then complains when they aren't the same. [*Rotary Realist*]

traffic light (*n.*) a device to get pedestrians halfway across the street in safety. [*anon.*]

tramp (*n.*) a ragged individualist. [*adapted from Jane Ace*]

treachery (*n.*) when someone thinks you are patting them on the back and you are actually drawing a bullseye. [*orig.*]

troublemaker (*n.*) a person who slips on the stairs and just before he dies, claims that someone pushed him. [*orig.*]

truce (*n.*) burying the hatchet but marking the spot. [*orig.*]

true love (*n.*) marrying the girl even though she doesn't have a steady job. [*G. Norman Collie*]

trust (*n.*) a financial speculation. [*Baudelaire*]

truth (*n.*) what you get from a politician who has given up all hope of becoming prime minister. [*orig.*]

absolute truth (*n.*) something that does not shift under pressure. [*orig.*]

twentieth century (*n.*) armaments, debt and planned obsolescence. [*adapted from Aldous Huxley*]

twentieth-century man (*n.*) one who lives within his means, but has to borrow the money to do it. [*orig.*]

twin exhaust (*n.*) teenager's mating call. [*adapted from J. A. Leary*]

twins (*n.*) the same kid twice. [*Dennis the Menace*]

tyranny (*n.*) general poverty relieved by occasional patriotic enthusiasm and maintained by terror. [*anon.*]

ukulele (n.) the missing link between music and noise. [*Professor E. K. Kruger*]

unbearable (*adj.*) a Christian with four aces. [*adapted from Oscar Wilde*]

university (n.) an institution for the postponement of experience. [*L. L. Levinson*]

upper crust (n.) a lot of crumbs held together by dough. [*Jean Webster*]

vacation (n.) time off to remind employees that the business can get along without them.
[*L. L. Levinson*]

vaccination (n.) a medical sacrament corresponding to baptism. [*Samuel Butler*]

vaccine (n.) a microbe with its face washed. [*Frank Scully*]

vacuum (n.) nothing shut up in a box. [*anon.*]

vacuum cleaner (n.) a broom with a stomach. [*anon.*]

vanity (n.) having an orgasm and shouting your own name. [*anon.*]

vegetarian (n.) someone who gives peas a chance. [*orig.*]

Venice (n.) a city that has become famous for its drains. [*orig.*]

verger (n.) a piece of church furniture. [*William Cowper*]

vinegar (n.) sour grapes. [*orig.*]

violin (n.) the revenge extracted by the intestines of a dead cat. [*anon.*]

virgin forest (n.) a forest in which the hand of man has never set foot. [*anon.*]

virtue (n.) a constant struggle against the laws of nature. [*De Finod*]

virus (n.) Latin for "Your guess is as good as mine." [*anon.*]

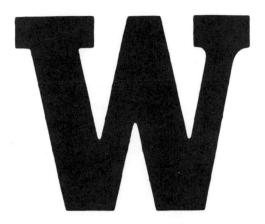

waffle (n.) a pancake with a non-skid sole. [anon.]

Wagner, Richard (n.) a composer with beautiful moments but awful half hours. [G. A. Rossini]

Wales (n.) a nation sick with inbreeding, worrying the carcass of an old song. [Reverend R. S. Thomas]

walking (n.) a means of transport to the garage. [anon.]

war (n.) the attractive rainbow that fades in showers of blood. [adapted from Abraham Lincoln]

wealth (n.) the sixth sense which enables you to enjoy the other five. [adapted from W. Somerset Maugham]

wedding (n.) a public confession of a private intention. [Ian Hay]

Western Australian (n.) a secessionist filled with beer and covered in sand. [orig.]

western civilisation (n.) alcohol, syphilis, trousers and the Bible. [Havelock Ellis]

wiener schnitzel (n.) (German) veal with a windcheater on. [orig.]

wife (n.) someone who can look in a drawer and find a pair of socks that aren't there. [anon.]

willpower (n.) being able to stop after eating one peanut. [Channing Pollock]

wisdom (n.) the comb life gives you after you have lost your hair. [Judith Stern]

wit (n.) a sword that is meant to make people feel the point as well as see it. [G. K. Chesterton]

witch (*n.*) a mother-in-law who made good. [*anon.*]

woman (*n.*) someone who has a wonderful sense of right and wrong but no sense of right and left. [*Don Herold*]

woman's intuition (*n.*) man's transparency. [*Joseph Cossman*]

women (*n.*) there are two types: those who have just had a baby and those who have just seen a lovely dress in the window. [*orig.*]

words (*n.*) things to kill time until our emotions render us inarticulate. [*Arthur Somers Roche*]

work (*n.*) a form of nervousness. [*Don Herold*]

worry (*n.*) interest paid on trouble before it falls due. [*W. R. Inge*]

writing (*n.*) the insatiable urge to scribble. [*adapted from William Gifford*]

wife . . . someone who can look in a drawer and find a pair of socks that aren't there.

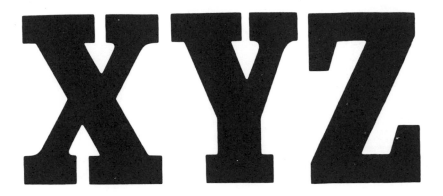

Xmas (*n.*) the celebration of consumer gullibility by the mass producers. [*orig.*]

yawn (*n.*) a silent shout. [*G. K. Chesterton*]

yes man (*n.*) someone who stoops to concur. [*Greta Christiansen*]

yoghurt (*n.*) milk emeritus. [*orig.*]

Yom Kippur (*n.*) (Hebrew) a Jewish herring. [*orig.*]

youth (*n.*) the confidence of 21. [*Samuel Johnson*]

Yugoslavia (*n.*) the Borneo of Europe. [*orig.*]

zealot (*n.*) a man with a strong taste for drink trying hard to keep sober. [*Elbert Hubbard*]

zig zag (*n.*) the shortest distance between two bars. [*L. L. Levinson*]

zoo (*n.*) an animal slum. [*Desmond Morris*]